# Fugitive Pigments

## Ruth Bavetta

FUTURECYCLE PRESS

*www.futurecycle.org*

Copyright © 2013 Ruth Bavetta
All Rights Reserved

Published by FutureCycle Press
Hayesville, North Carolina, USA

ISBN 978-1-938853-31-9

# Contents

## Memories Suspended by Filaments

Memories Suspended by Filaments......................................................9
Photograph of My Father................................................................11
Dear as Salt.....................................................................................12
Black, White...................................................................................14
Landscape with Spool of Thread....................................................15
Atelier.............................................................................................16
Drawing Lessons from the Past......................................................17
List Found in a Copy Machine......................................................18
Edna Rosalie...................................................................................19
What Cannot Save Us....................................................................20
What Is Left to Show That I Was Here?.......................................21

## Colors and Outlines

Colors and Outlines.......................................................................25
Still Life with Pencil......................................................................26
Drawing Conclusions.....................................................................27
Vanitas............................................................................................28
Red.................................................................................................29
Bay..................................................................................................30
Fog..................................................................................................31
Hot Breath on a Bitter Night........................................................32
Running Fence...............................................................................33
To Make a Mark............................................................................34
Perspective......................................................................................35
What You Should Know About Shadows....................................36

## Gathering

First Lesson....................................................................................39
Imagine..........................................................................................40
The Old Woman............................................................................41
Gathering.......................................................................................43
Given Forms..................................................................................44

How to Create an Exquisite Corpse.................................................45
Instructions for the Day.................................................................46
The Annunciation..........................................................................47
The Color of Wind........................................................................ 48
Adagio............................................................................................49
When the Room Fades..................................................................50
Luncheon on the Grass.................................................................. 51

## Imaging the Heart

Self-Portrait with Still Life............................................................. 55
Salt Water...................................................................................... 56
Smoke............................................................................................ 57
Message......................................................................................... 58
Consider as Large Drawing............................................................ 59
Beacon........................................................................................... 60
Camera degli Sposi (The Bridal Chamber)....................................61
Blood Test..................................................................................... 63
Imaging the Heart......................................................................... 64
A Cappella.....................................................................................66
Self-Portrait................................................................................... 67

Acknowledgments......................................................................... 69

*for Leif*

# Memories Suspended by Filaments

∞

# Memories Suspended by Filaments

*in the voice of Joseph Cornell*

The house is small, but it has room for dreams.
For birds, books, stamps, stars, marbles, butterflies,
balls, dolls, my brother Robert, maps, romance,
playing cards, lace, lobsters, small sticky hope.

Eyes down, I walk the streets of Manhattan,
eat pastries, sweet, stale, talk to pigeons, find
orphaned desires in gutters, in dime stores,
in second-hand shops with dusty windows.

I discover, gather, magpie away.
My treasures hibernate, waiting, sleeping
in basement shelf rows, labeled by heartbeats
slowed to a drip. When my dossiers have lived

together long enough, I take them out,
let them speak, cherish them in my boxes,
where parrots talk of sunsets, and clay pipes
float and fill with a summer of bubbles.

Behind glass, my birds and my women sing,
locked into universes I create,
where lovers are dancers, princesses, queens,
secrets detained in shining glass bottles.

I sing the *juene fille* Lauren Bacall,
slender Botticelli, silent in blue,
construct a pink palace with sapphire stars.
I mediate history for the Prince

of the Medici, give him a compass
so he finds and he follows true love. Oh,
Bebe Marie, you are so beautiful,
pale pink, hidden among silvery twigs.

## Photograph of My Father

He sits in shadow, without a sign
of movement, powerless
against the current
that has carried him thus far.

At the edge of the porch,
corn lilies wither in the grass.
In the kitchen, cabinets of glass,
painted pottery, pots of wheat.

Fate has skewed his neurons,
drained away the loose change
of motion. Synapses
have somehow got the address wrong,

vanished like thoughts unspun.
His eyes are closed,
but the chime of his life beats softly on,
dry as the blaze of stars.

# Dear as Salt

*on Ralph Going's painting, Double Ketchup, 1996-97*

The salt stands iconic on the counter
guardianed by blood-red double ketchups,
flooded with light flowing from the right.

Sodium chloride, a molecule of two,
each harmful alone, when bonded
together they live in harmony.

Halite, hexoctahedral, isometric, perfect
cleavage. Here are pure white cubic crystals
sparkling in a stubby glass shaker

on a diner counter. Sought and sold for seasoning,
medicine, taxes, ketchup, the mining of silver.
Preservative for Egypt's everlasting dead.

The Princess told her father,
you are as dear to me as salt
and he, offended to be compared

to such a commonplace, threatened
to banish her from the palace. Until
she served him roast bream and darioles,

mustard soup, simnel cake, Swithin cream,
pasties filled with marrow, all without salt,
tasteless as a life without love.

Salt makes it harder for things to boil
and harder too, for them to freeze,
prevents the yeast from overflowing.

From mines, from brines, from solar heat,
symbol of fertility, symbol of purity,
regulator of the heart.

Salt is ancient, salt is eternal.
Salt is what he offers me
every night across the table.

# Black, White

*homage to Cesar Vallejo*

He died, my father,
in Auburn, on a Wednesday
in January, with the blankets thin
and white as his bones, unable
to turn to the fourth floor window,
unable to see the freezing clouds.

He died, my father,
after he could not swallow the sweetness
of the pears, after refusing
the yellow pill and the green one,
after the priest he did not want
came anyway.

He died, and he lies
high on Mill Peak,
black ash, white snow.

# Landscape with Spool of Thread

Three cool stars,
a California beach,
a summer radio,
words like "please"
and "forever."
Clouds turned pink
with longing,
hair tangled with sand,
my grandmother's jade ring
lost under the seat
of a parked car.

# Atelier

*for my grandmother, Edna Rosalie Tuttle Pomeroy*

*Turpentine*
*mineral spirits*
*casein*
*glycerin*
Let me go to her
in memory, watch
her prepare the canvas.
*gesso*
*fresco*
*lead white*
*graphite*
In the aftertimes,
she's a last dream
*rose madder*
before waking.
*cerulean*
*cadmium*
*cobalt*
High at the window,
morning
*glazing*
the apple,
and in her studio,
*porcelain enamel*
her first cup of tea.

# Drawing Lessons from the Past

Consider a series of drawings
in which one thing changes
to another. Start
with shapes that are akin—
body unites with chair, bee
becomes airliner, mingling
sting with jet propulsion.

Villages distill to fields, daffodils
are crocodiles. When at last
it seems that changes are nothing more
than rearrangements, kings
will willingly transform to knaves,
children can be turned to slaves,
townsfolk mutate into thieves.

Cities, almost on their own, unknit
themselves to plains, books
can be defined as flames,
synagogues succumb
to trains. A people
will dissolve to smoke.

## List Found in a Copy Machine

Another tree
More houses
More railroads
Another star

# Edna Rosalie

Before she was my grandmother,
did John Sloan lean over her shoulder to guide
her hand at the Art Student's League?
Did she take tea with Robert Henri?

I wish I could talk with her now
about the golden mean; ask if her husband
demanded the divorce or if she threw him out;
discuss raking light and the angels of Raphael.

Did the young chauffeur salve her heart?
In her back garden, did she sometimes lean
on her rosewood crutches and dream?
Was there never another man?

If I took tea with her now,
we could discuss the use of cerulean blue,
ultramarine, rose madder—that fugitive
pigment. She could tell me why

she let her canvases warp,
her paints dry up.
I could tell her she was right
about the use of black.

## What Cannot Save Us

The graveyard of shelves,
paintings, old pearls and gloves,
shoes that have become too small.

Soft leaves, green lakes,
faded linen, oranges, cloves,
a smooth round stone.

Poppies beyond the road, nettles
at the gate, cabinets crammed
with china, the steady pace of blood.

The ivy that kills the tree
when there is nothing left.

# What Is Left to Show That I Was Here?

Remember me in the Ultramarine
of an empty bed, find me
in the Cardinal Purple
of a canceled stamp, the Marking Blue
of builders, handsaws, teachers. Viridian
of rooms webbed with birds.
I will be in the Cadmium Red
of random apples, in the Burnt
Umber basket of a shadow. Vermilion
will account for a puncture
in the skin of loneliness.
Look for me in the Aurelian pollen
of Cerulean lilacs, in the ache
of Mars Violet. Bone Black crows
on branches, Alizarin Crimson to weep
and soak my shirt.
Lamp Black.
Cardinal Purple.
Caput Mortuum.

# Colors and Outlines

# Colors and Outlines

*for Ann*

Ever since the last
biopsy, she has known
she is not safe, has never
been safe, from the invisible
procession of cells.
Since that day, when the ache
passed from the imaginary
to the real, she has been naked
beneath her skin.

The newspaper, carelessly flung
near her mailbox, brings reports
she cannot read. She counts
only April speeding past. Her last
pennies are about to be spent.
She will let them go
as she has let go of the desire
to get into her car
and just keep driving.

## Still Life with Pencil

The book
you were reading last night,
the old green flashlight
your grandmother kept
under her pillow,
the carving knife
bought by your former husband—
look how your fingers
curl around them. The key
to your first house,
a beautiful but empty pen,
the ball of the thumb
you have taken for granted
your entire life, the astonishing curve
of your fingernails. These are the things
you will draw from.

# Drawing Conclusions

Instead of touching his hand,
I ran my finger along the edge
of my sketchbook. "I need
to know where I stand."

He turned the sketchbook
and leafed through the pages,
stopping at a drawing I'd done
of my own hands breaking an egg.
"That's good," he said.

## Vanitas

A blind drawing
of an eggbeater,
a shoe, a watch
with a band that curls;
a soft purse, a knapsack;
a collection of keys
to a house
you've never entered;
a small branch
that leafed out
the year you were sixteen;
a glove
worn by someone
you loved;
your hand
lying open on the table.

# Red

is a broken pomegranate
spilling blood and rubies
onto salt-white linen;

a shattered glass of burgundy;
maraschino cherries,
the sticky lips
of a teenage siren.

It is a Chinese leather box,
a Hungarian Rhapsody,
the taste of sachertorte,
a spill of rouge
in a dim and shuttered room.

# Bay

*Claire Browne, 2000, colored pencil on canvas*

She draws tiny circles one by one with her left hand.
They foam across the canvas like bubbles on the beach
roil and effervesce across the sand.

Colored pencil circles done freehand
on gesso sanded clean and white as bleach,
drawn one by one with her left hand.

A mitosis of new cells, bacteria, a strand
of stars, thousands come together, leach
their efflorescence from the sand.

A spume of blues and greens fanned
as distant from the past as she can reach
drawing round and round with her left hand.

Creeping over bounds and edges, contraband
reflections crawl across the canvas, pleached
with roils and effervescence on the sand.

She transcends a childhood she did not understand,
closes memories away without their speech,
as tiny circles fall one by one from her left hand
and they roil and effloresce across the sand.

# Fog

A ghost in the chaparral,
the grey breath of its face
a last sweet scent of sage,
cool, blue, dim.
Pale cambric
fanned like feathers
across dark hills, trailing silently
through the open window,
curling among teacups,
dictionaries, clean sheets. Absence
is gigantic, bottomless
as a single drop of water.

## Hot Breath on a Bitter Night

Flames, each a jagged sleeve of silk,
fling desperate arms
across the hills,
tiger-colored waves
like ghostly horses.
Malicious glints
bright as polished knives,
a cosmic urgency run amok,
in a chance course
of feverish light.
A blind slash clinging
to the edges of the world.

# Running Fence

*Christo, Sonoma County, California, 1976*

Improbable as a line of laundry,
indispensable as a spine,
a lightning bolt
that celebrates the contour of hills,
it fades into fog, rises into sun.
A dash of chalk against the summer brown,
describing the wind,
it disappears into a valley, reappears
on the hill, curves
over a crest, gone,
returned
to plunge
at last
into the sea.

## To Make a Mark

Emptiness is deadly. To master it
you must blemish it. A long slashing
line, a curve curling back
upon itself, a line that winds
with no end in mind.

Once you have destroyed perfection
you will be entering
a country you have not known.
I will not tell you this.

You may find something amazing—
someone to take your hand, a waterfall,
a fall from three flights up.
I will not tell you this, either.

I will tell you only that it doesn't matter
if, by the end, your first mark
has disappeared. It matters only
that you have made it.
Pick up your pencil now.
Begin.

# Perspective

The long faint
wail of the train
in the canyon, a vocable
pulled to a vanishing point.

Beyond the brilliant
green of the willows,
a scrim of fog
where all parallel lines

converge on a single horizon
always determined
by where I am. Even if
it is hidden is by trees,

mountains, walls, clouds,
sorrow, it is always there.
I will never see beyond it.
I want you to listen.

I want you to see.
Before the changing shores
of shadow, a single lemon hangs
like a lamp of gold.

## What You Should Know About Shadows

A line cannot contain the edge
between light and dark.
When we were in the sunshine
we were clear. Our shadows
vanished at midday and stretched
in the raking light of afternoon.
But when the light began to dim,
the borders blurred. Shadows
are darkest near their source.

A shadow takes the shape
of what casts it. A rose
is not an ambulance.
Complex ground distorts
and fractures what falls on it,
sometimes beyond knowing.
When our shadows crossed,
they became the sum
of two darknesses.

# Gathering

∞

## First Lesson

Even Rembrandt's paintings
didn't all end up in a museum.
Some he scraped off and painted over.
Others he pitched into the canal,
along with his debts and bad teeth.
But the debts recurred,
the teeth gave him bad breath,
the canal gurgled and disturbed his sleep.

Picasso drew on napkins to pay his bar tab.
But even when he worked on hot-pressed,
acid-free, pure linen paper,
he sometimes trampled his drawings
or folded them into airplanes
to sail at the heads of his wives and mistresses.

Leonardo couldn't get the smile right.
Not the first time. Nor the second.
Georgia painted a world of bones,
deserts, and high, wide spaces—
and a world of paintings
she should have had the sense to burn.

Van Gogh's early drawings
were stiff and awkward—
no coiling sunflowers, no writhing skies,
no cypresses twisting toward the stars.
Did you think this was going to be easy?

## Imagine

walking up forty-two stairs,
the smell of a rubber ball, your arm
brushing against a stucco wall,
the prick of a pin in the tip
of your right index finger.

There was a clock you once knew;
draw its tick inside your body.
There was a bicycle on a dirt road
the summer you fell in love;
balance on its handlebars.

Enter a room you have forgotten.
Walk through midnight
carrying a make-believe lantern.
Stretch out your hand,
touch the horizon.

# The Old Woman

When I go into my studio,
I see the old woman
sitting in her chair,
hands clasped, waiting.
I walk past her,

take out the pale wood frame
I glued together last week,
painted with two coats of varnish,
sanding after each coat,
rubbing it smooth with steel wool.

The old woman is turned away
gazing into the distance.
I place the frame face down,
clean the glass and lay it in.
I place the mat over the glass.
The drawing goes face down
over the mat. Next, barrier paper,
finally the foamboard backing.

I don't even know who she is.
She could even be dead by now.
I squeeze brads into the frame
to hold in the package,
add screw eyes and picture wire.

When I turn the frame over,
I see the old woman again,
at least eighty years since
she was born, a good ten years

since I photographed her. Three years
since I made the drawing.
I have her at last, safe
under glass.

## Gathering

We gather together beneath the clouds,
ahead of the gathering storm,
weaving dreams from light and air,
silky mohair, fine merino,
cashmere from Kashmiri goats.

Collecting lilacs, lavender, roses,
black-eyed Susans, Shasta daisies
with golden eyes.
Shall we gather at the river?

Reaping wheat for daily bread,
harvesting sweet corn. Oats, peas,
beans and barley grow. Rye whiskey,
rye whiskey, rye whiskey I cry.

Collecting salty seashells
at the salty seashore, mussels,
rock oysters, Sozon's cones,
owl-eyed limpets. Angel wings.

# Given Forms

Cracks
in the driveway.
My father
doing crosswords
on the porch. My mother
shuffling from room
to room. Summer
hot and thick as blood,
sky heavy as draperies.
The iron bedframe.
The ladder still there.
A hawk.

## How to Create an Exquisite Corpse

We come together
in the night between two wars,
taste words— the dormitory
of friable girls puts the odious box aright—
listen to images.

Munich, Paris, Zurich.
Tristan Tzara, Joan Miró, Man Ray,
Yves Tanguy, André Breton.

We pass out paper,
fold each sheet into sections.
The lubricious toad defrauds
the incendiary onion.

Andy will begin the drawing, fold
the paper, hand it to Tristan
who will try to sneak in words—
the Senegal oyster, perhaps,
or the tricolored thunderclap.

Tell him to stop, connect
his drawing to Man's,
pass the paper to Andy.

And so on.

And so on.

Lean forward with us.
Kiss the exquisite corpse
on his cold and careless cheek.

## Instructions for the Day

Take with you
what you will need,
leave by the north exit
or the south,
then turn
either east or west.
When you come
to the corner
turn left or right
or continue straight
until you come to a dead end,
then stop
and look around.
This is the place
you must draw from.

# The Annunciation

*Simone Martini, 1333*

Mary twists to stare at the intruder,
an Angel, no less. His plaid-lined cape
flutters, lifted by a breeze
that touches nothing else. Waxy lilies,
white and virginal, spring from a vase.

She turns away, clutches her robe
of ultramarine and gold across her breast
as if she's been caught undressed.
She's stuck her thumb into her book
so she won't lose her place.
Her mouth turns down.

She sees it even now— the birth out of town
in dismal lodgings, swaddling clothes, damp
and odorous, husband resentful
of a child not his own, the embarrassing ruckus
in the temple, the motley gang of followers,
the agonizing and ignominious death,
the sponge soaked in vinegar.

## The Color of Wind

Feel the softness
of Thursday, revel in its pink.
Smell the late summer moonlight.

Listen to the green
of the bell. Taste
the bitterness of blue,
the sweetness of the sun.

See the sound
of the harpsichord, listen
to yellow, sing the song
of the stone, tremble
at its touch.

# Adagio

A slow stroll eased
into three syllables, not four,
for G and I are married

into one soft sound.

A sweet plum
of a word, slide it

across the spoon
of your tongue.

Let it repeat,

a bell slowly tolling from beyond
three valleys, carrying

a calm the color of gold dust.

Slide into the susurrus
of faraway surf.

Pianissimo, pianissimo.

## When the Room Fades

I want the orange felt hat,
the silver brush, the notebook
with the broken back.
I want Los Angeles, Encino,
San Bernardino, the overflow
of pages, the tangle of pins,
all those things I've carried
wrapped in the silk of living.

I want the shoes, sunglasses,
broken seashells, the lilies,
lawns and clotheslines.
The slow decay
of lilacs, swift summer
stars against a sinking sky.
I want just one single minute
to carry like a peach pit
in my deepest pocket.

# Luncheon on the Grass

*Eduard Manet, 1863*

Two young men
lounge on the grass,
black jackets, spotless trousers.
Next to them, a naked woman.

Another woman, wearing only
her shimmy, dabbles in the pond.
Picnic basket, overturned,
spills ripe fruit, golden bread.

The men absorbed in discussion—
philosophy, stock market, horses—
haven't even removed their cravats
or tasted the food the women brought.

The naked woman's feet are muddy,
perhaps she's just come from a dip
beside her sister. Instead of listening
to the men, she stares out at us.

So? She says, when was your last picnic?
When did you last strip down
and turn your muddy feet to view?
In a minute, she'll reach out
and bite into one of those peaches.

# Imaging the Heart

∞

## Self-Portrait with Still Life

The watch that was my grandmother's,
lost in the gym in junior high,
the Phi Beta Kappa key
I wasn't supposed to flaunt, but did,
books spilling off the table, tubes of paint
hardening in a drawer, a piano lost in a fire,
a guitar gone out of tune,
all of them, almost within reach.

Broken seashells carted coast to coast,
the long red nightgown
bought for our first night together,
a bowl of oranges—there, in the kitchen window.
I can see them, almost touch them,

## Salt Water

I do not know these hands
that fumble buttons, tremble
threading needles, struggle
to arrange pieces of the puzzle.
Shards of terracotta,
peeling concrete walls.

I do, however, recognize
the fingers, long and crooked,
with the dark knuckles that so embarrassed
me when I was young
that every night I scrubbed them
with the nail brush.
Sadness of salt-washed rocks,
elegance of seaweed.

A half moon rises on each fingernail.
Waves wash across the beach,
climb the strand, scaling
the seawall, lapping the cliff.

# Smoke

From the ordered flight of the Canada geese
I've learned to gather thoughts in rows,
coinage of the not-yet-wholly-awakened day.
From the murmurous churn of the train
on the Feather River Route to Winnemucca
I've become skilled in the consolation of solitude.
From the fringe of trees across the meadow,
I know the thin blue scrim
filtering over Eureka Ridge. From the dead trees,
on the burned-out slope, I've learned the scar
on my breast, the ashes on my tongue,
and the slow fires trailing.

# Message

As I was dancing on the roof, the shingles stirred
and turned to sand and water filled the sky. Drunk
with hope, I unfurled my wings, leapt far
into the canyon, where I lay on speckled stones.

Golden perch swam from the sagebrush
to nibble at my ankles with delicate silver teeth.
When I touched the largest fish, its shining scales
burned my finger to bleached and barren bone.

As the tide spun toward the shore and waves sang open
the gates of trees, I reached out with my bonefinger
and wrote my testimony on the sand.

# Consider as Large Drawing

Your hands
washing the coffeepot,
writing a check,
peeling an orange,
touching the cheek
of your lover. Holding

your grandmother's cameo,
the key to your house,
your divorce papers,
your certificate
for perfect attendance.

Use nothing but line
that goes from thick to thin,
from dark to light.

No shading.

# Beacon

I am the rain
washing away the moon,
the rescue helicopter's bottom rung
dangling like a chain of light.
I am dark kitchens,
violins and pomegranates,
the box of chocolate cherries,
a torn petticoat rimmed with lace.
I live in the unspiraling fern,
in summer thunder, in the seed
of sweet alyssum asleep
in warming soil, the heron standing
in the neighbor's dog yard.

# Camera degli Sposi (The Bridal Chamber)

*ceiling fresco, Andrea Mantegna, 1474*

Afterwards, we lie on the bed,
limbs flung wide, my kirtle, his *doppieto*
on the floor, tangled with the wedding
silks, our sweaty bodies far apart,

breathing hard, but not in unison.
The ceiling above me is a painted balustrade
around a painted hole, a painted sky
strewn with painted clouds.

It's like being at the bottom of a well.
Outside, it could be raining—
lightning, thunder, stars darkening—
but in this room the sky is always blue.

What a crowd up there around the edge—
all those merry cherubs, a dark man in a turban,
several women staring, even a bird.
I feel like I should cover up.

The cherubs have fat, creased thighs,
stubby little penises. The man cocks
his head. The bird gazes at the clouds,
as if overtaken by yearning.

Below, on rumpled sheets
of fine-woven linen, I touch his shoulder.
That bird, I ask, is it a pheasant?
He looks, rolls away from me.

*Idiota,* he says, it's a peacock.
I want to stroke the soft hair
curling at the back of his neck,
but I don't dare. Instead I look up.

On the balustrade,
between two women, is a heavy tub
filled with greenery, balanced
on the very edge.

## Blood Test

I could describe how sunlight
reflects off the leaves of the orange tree
outside my window or the fox

I see every night as he heads around
the corner of the house,

the rhododendrons that died for want
of water, mountains dark
against pale sky,

the highway snaking
the pass, trailing headlights

in the night, shoes abandoned
on the sand years ago
when it was summer.

The technician sticks the needle
into my vein and the blood
bubbles out, dark and red.

## Imaging the Heart

*Echocardiogram: a test that delineates the deep structures of the heart by the use of high-frequency sound waves.*

The technician pulls a curtain,
tells me to get undressed,
lie on the table.
I can leave my watch on.
She sticks small sensors
on my ribs below my breast.
Western sun and butterscotch,
smell of sage in summer.

*Cardiograph: an instrument that registers graphically the movements of the heart.*

She lowers the lights,
turns on the machine.
The screen is black.
Crackerjack, Mozart, new-mown lawns.
Presses my chest with the wand,
taps the computer keys—
my heart in black and white.
Salt smell of the sea,
crisp, clean sheets.

*Imaging: making or producing a likeness; to vividly evoke.*

Hilltops with views,
sprinklers on a hot sidewalk.
She touches another key.
My heart—red, juicy,
pulsing and flopping.

Sixty seven years without stopping,
the valves fluttering,
opening and shutting.
Deer behind the shadows,
a mockingbird at midnight.

*Echo: repetition by reflection of waves from a surface; a remnant or vestige.*

Early mornings blurred by fog,
waves slapping against the sand.
Tapping the keyboard again,
turning the wand, seeking.
Blue lightning streaks the screen.
Artifacts, says the technician,
pushing harder with the wand.
My husband's warm hands.

## A Cappella

You are a small seashell,
white as my heart.
I carry you around
like a song in my pocket.

Think of a bird
dancing in the dark,
the pale rain flashing,
the small high clouds.

The wind falls,
luxurious with leaves.
You are the pond
that is my home.

# Self-Portrait

*Alice Neel, 1980, oil on canvas*

Eighty you are, Alice, planted
in a blue-striped chair, more naked
than nude. In one hand you hold a brush
like a baton, as if conducting your life;
in the other, a rag for wiping out mistakes.

Your breasts, like mine, droop
over an abdomen poured like a land slump
onto plump thighs. Pizza, pregnancies,
peanut butter, whiskey, long sweet afternoons
in the studio instead of in the gym.

Turkey neck, jowls, marriage, divorce,
paint under the fingernails. I see myself
with the same down-turned mouth,
the same skeptical stare, and wonder
how we got our bodies through it all.

You used to say an empty chair by the window
would be your only self-portrait. Save
that chair for me, Alice. I'm drawing close.
Tell me how to come ashore.

# Acknowledgments

Grateful acknowledgement is made to the following publications in which certain poems in this collection first appeared, sometimes in slightly different form.

*IthacaLit:* "Black, White"
*Poetry Quarterly:* "What Is Left to Show That I Was Here?"
*Spillway:* "List Found in a Copy Machine"
*The Writer:* "Red"
*Zone International Journal of Prose and Poetry:* "Imagine"
*Sugar House Review:* "How to Create an Exquisite Corpse"
*Chiron Review:* "Instructions for the Day"
*Blood and Thunder:* "Imaging the Heart"

*Cover art, "Summer Promises," by Ruth Bavetta (www.ruthbavetta.com); author photo by Beth Beeman; cover and interior book design by Diane Kistner (dkistner@futurecycle.org); Adobe Garamond Pro text with Grenoble Serial titling*

# About FutureCycle Press

FutureCycle Press is dedicated to publishing lasting English-language poetry and flash fiction books, chapbooks, and anthologies in both print-on-demand and ebook formats. Founded in 2007 by long-time independent editor/publishers and partners Diane Kistner and Robert S. King, the press incorporated as a nonprofit in 2012. A number of our editors are distinguished poets and authors in their own right, and we have been actively involved in the small press movement going back to the early seventies.

The FutureCycle Poetry Book Prize and honorarium is awarded annually for the best full-length volume of poetry we publish in a calendar year. Introduced in 2013, our Good Works projects are devoted to issues of global significance, with all proceeds donated to a related worthy cause. We are dedicated to giving all authors we publish the care their work deserves, making our catalog of titles the most distinguished it can be, and paying forward any earnings to fund more great books.

We've learned a few things about independent publishing over the years. We've also evolved a unique, resilient publishing model that allows us to focus mainly on vetting and preserving for posterity the most books of exceptional quality without becoming overwhelmed with bookkeeping and mailing, fundraising activities, or taxing editorial and production "bubbles." To find out more about what we are doing, come see us at www.futurecycle.org.

## The FutureCycle Poetry Book Prize

All full-length volumes of poetry published by FutureCycle Press in a given calendar year are considered for the annual FutureCycle Poetry Book Prize. This allows us to consider each submission on its own merits, outside of the context of a contest. Too, the judges see the finished book, which will have benefitted from the beautiful book design and strong editorial gloss we are famous for.

The book ranked the best in judging is announced as the prize-winner in the subsequent year. There is no fixed monetary award; instead, the winning poet receives an honorarium of 20% of the total net royalties from all poetry books and chapbooks the press sold online in the year the winning book was published. The winner is also accorded the honor of judging the next year's competition.

www.ingramcontent.com/pod-product-compliance
Lightning Source LLC
LaVergne TN
LVHW020938090426
835512LV00020B/3419